About the Book

In 2003, we sat down together to write our first book, **The Progression of Wealth.**® That book has since guided thousands of people to financial independence and has arguably started the movement in holistic, goals-based financial planning and wealth management.

But after you spend years working to establish your wealth, how do you maintain it— and more importantly, enjoy it— throughout your retirement?

How can you continue to maintain your lifestyle?

How can you ensure your family will be cared for?

This book will show you how. The strategies and knowledge presented within will help you plan and invest so you're prepared for both the expected and unexpected in retirement. So many people view retirement as a time to cut back and reign in their finances; we see it as a time to celebrate maintaining the lifestyle you enjoy for your entire life. Our methodology will give you peace of mind knowing your assets are properly allocated, structured, and protected. You will never have to worry about your financial comfort again because it will be taken care of.

THE
PROGRESSION
OF WEALTH®

THE PROGRESSION OF WEALTH

How to Build and Protect Your Retirement With Confidence

JAY L. HELLER, CPA & BRIAN KOHUTE, CPA

Printed in the United States of America

ISBN Hardcover: 978-0-692-59270-0
ISBN eBook: 978-0-692-59269-4

Library of Congress Control Number: 2015957678

Cover Design: Chuck Maciunas
Interior Design: Ghislain Viau

*Dedicated to our loyal clients, our loving families,
and our tremendous team at Meridian Wealth Partners.*

Table of Contents

CHAPTER 1

Is Retirement the Land of Confusion?

*K*aren, a senior human resources executive at a large corporation, is married to Curt, the owner of a technology company. Together they make a good living, but they feel like they never have enough money. Retirement is soon approaching, and Curt and Karen have dreams—dreams of travel, the ability to pick up new hobbies, and maybe even the purchase of a house on the beach at which their family vacations every year. Their children are grown, and when the time comes, they want to be able to help their grandchildren too. But they worry about whether they can ever turn those dreams into reality.

*****

Thousands of families across the country find themselves in Karen and Curt's situation. They work hard and earn what should be more than an ample salary to meet their financial goals, yet nevertheless find themselves uncomfortable financially, all the while wondering where it all went—and what will become of their future

The truth is, Karen and Curt have everything they need to achieve their financial goals—to provide for their family, to enjoy their retirement—except one key component: a Blueprint™ to build milestones in order to turn their dreams into reality. Without such a Blueprint, their progress toward financial independence is more like living in a Fragmented Finance Trap™. People who fall into this kind of trap tend to have certain things in common: they don't have clear goals or a plan to achieve them, their investments are disorganized, and they may be under- or over-insured. They may be taking too much investment risk for the potential reward ... or they may not be investing enough. Like many people who fall into Fragmented Finance Traps, Karen and Curt may be relying too much on company stock and failing to take full advantage of other benefits Karen's employer may offer. They are paying too much in taxes, and their many financial advisors are not communicating with one another and coordinating their activities.

Planning is the life source of your financial independence, and even more so, of your successful retirement. Your retirement years are the time in your life when you are no longer contributing money to savings; instead, you are drawing money out and spending it down. How you choose to spend it—whether on yourself, your family, a charitable cause you believe in, or all of the above—is entirely up to you.

We all dream about retirement, and we each have a unique vision of what we want our retirement to look like. Perhaps you envision you and your spouse traveling the globe and exploring the great cities of the world. Maybe you've always wanted to spend the summer in Europe. Or it could be that your dreams are simply to spend more time with family and friends, to help children and grandchildren and donate more time to your local community, or volunteer for a cause that is dear to you.

Whatever your particular retirement dream may involve, you, like Karen and Curt, will need to develop a retirement strategy that will enable you to achieve your goals. Without a strategy, you'll be wandering in the desert, perpetually uncertain if you have established enough financial security to live out your dreams.

Perhaps you've already reached retirement, and you were well prepared. You have worked hard. You saved and invested like you were told to do. You may feel like you

3

planned effectively for a secure future, but you may still be wondering, *Will it be enough?*

Will you honestly have enough money to retire and realize your dreams without giving up your current lifestyle? Or will you have to pare down aspects of your lifestyle?

Worst-case scenario: Will you be forced to completely excise certain dreams?

For many, this is the question that keeps us awake at night, and disturbs our sense of peace when the subject arises. This uncertainty is normal. You are not alone with your concerns. It can be very confusing when you think of retirement planning in grand terms. There are so many things to consider, and the sheer number of options can become overwhelming and paralyzing. The key is to break down the planning into smaller parts.

Common Retirement Goals

If you take it one step at a time, and truly seek to understand the concepts as you put a plan together, it will seem less daunting.

Below is a list of the most common goals people share with us.

- Continuing to enjoy your current lifestyle for your entire retirement
- Protecting your family

- Planning for the unexpected
- Pursuing a new hobby or activity
- Planning for potential health concerns
- Traveling to places you always wanted to visit
- Contributing your time and resources to charitable causes
- Leaving a legacy

Retiring successfully depends on many different factors. However, the majority of people who find themselves unable to retire comfortably simply failed to address these goals early on.

The primary purpose of planning is to ensure that both you and your loved ones will be cared for according to your wishes. It can give you the security of knowing that, come what may, you will never become dependent upon another person for your care and wellbeing. It can direct how your assets are distributed. Estate planning provides for family security, business succession, management of your assets, and the nomination of a guardian for your minor children. A proper estate plan can also help to reduce the cost of probate later on.

The important thing to remember is that once you reach your retirement, you should not, for any reason, allow the financial security of your family to be subject to unnecessary risk, taxes, or fees, or to be mismanaged due to little or no planning. The last thing your family should have to deal with in a time of grief is being hit with the costs of legalities, family squabbling, and financial stress.

Proper planning today can assure not only that your personal wishes are satisfied, but also that your family remains as strong without you as they were with you. This is one of the best gifts you could give them: having the foresight to take care of your affairs before they are forced to do so themselves. We have worked with so many people who find themselves sorting through their parents' or spouse's finances in an already stressful time, which only compounds their sense of loss.

So how do you plan?

Planning takes time and research, along with a close assessment of your current financial situation, available assets, income and expenses, and your retirement goals.

Men and women have different financial goals. Have you ever really sat down and discussed what matters to your spouse or partner? Are your retirement goals aligned? If you can determine what is important to you—to buy a second home, to travel the world, to help your grandkids with their education—and then define a set of goals to help you achieve it, then you will be much more empowered to create a financial plan.

The accumulation of wealth alone is not the goal. Rather, wealth is a means to a better, more meaningful life. The more you know about what makes life meaningful to you, the better you can plan to achieve it. By opening the lines of communication about this often- uncomfortable topic, you will begin to develop an idea of which areas need to be addressed, and how to go about developing a comprehensive retirement plan.

We have found that those who fall short of their retirement goals or experience stress as retirement approaches only do so because of their lack of planning. Many consider retirement planning a one-time deal, rather than an ongoing process. Humans are not intrinsically disciplined for investing for retirement. In fact, Benjamin Graham, the "Father of Value Investing" and mentor to Warren Buffett is quoted as saying, "The investor's chief problem, and even his worst enemy, is likely to be himself."

The unique proposition about moving into retirement is that you've gathered a formidable expanse of life experience, and the more life you experience, the more your needs and tastes can evolve. What you may have planned before that has worked for you, may not work now. Transitioning into retirement calls for a transition in the way you manage your assets, as well as the financial goals you have in place. But knowing where to begin, or what direction to take, is often the first obstacle. You may know what you value, or the goals you'd like to achieve, but how exactly do you get there?

Every day we are exposed to so much market information, industry opinion, and advertising that we wind up doubting our financial decisions. We often react to what we see on the TV or what our friends are telling us about this or that stock, instead of maintaining our focus on those elements we *can* control. Many investors are too eager to follow their emotions or the advice of others who may also be acting on emotion or incomplete information.

We have been guiding clients through the complex maze of retirement planning and wealth management for many years. We've developed a flexible planning process called The Progression of Wealth® that will guide you through the complexity of financial planning. We don't act on emotion, and we make sure you are fully informed and on board before making any decision, big or small, with your money.

Our Story

In 1980, Jay Heller started his own accounting firm, and for the next twenty-five years, he prepared thousands of tax returns and worked with hundreds of small-business owners and corporate executives.

Despite Jay's clients' business success, many of them were not well educated or prepared when it came to their personal finances and retirement planning.

With his client experiences, Jay made it his life goal to help people financially plan for retirement and manage their finances during retirement.

About this time, Jay met Brian Kohute and found in him a common vision of educating clients and advocating for their personal finances. We were both trained CPAs and were frustrated by how financial services were being sold as products without the education and "service" components. The only way consumers could get advice was by buying products, and often these products did more to boost the company's profits than to build the consumer's financial security. These advisors were often no more than salespeople interested in earning a commission. The relationship was only as strong as the ability of the consumer to buy more and more products.

We founded our own wealth firm in order to overcome these problems. Our goal has always been to become activists for our clients' long-term financial comfort and security.

Drawing from decades of experience, we developed a systematic discipline to connect the management of wealth with meaningful personal goals. These ideas came together as our first book, *The Progression of Wealth*®, which received attention in the national press. In the years since, these same ideas have been the subject of industry seminars for financial professionals, stimulating an ongoing discussion of best practices in the financial planning world, and have been the planning practices we use with all our clients.

Today, we call our model "The Progression of Wealth®." For us, this emphasizes the long-term commitment required to succeed financially. It isn't an overnight arrival, nor is it a hop, skip, and a jump to the finish line. Acquiring and sustaining wealth is a gradual progression, one that requires a considerable amount of thought and planning.

The Progression of Wealth is a process that takes a comprehensive approach to financial planning and encompasses all aspects of retirement life, always with the goal of sustainability. Using The Progression of Wealth process, everything will be in place and everyone will have peace of mind. In short, it's how you can take the unnecessary worry out of your retirement. Because if you spend all your golden years worrying, they're not very golden at all.

This book is our attempt to help you retire successfully. Within these pages, you'll learn about our in-depth process to creating a successful retirement. You'll see The Progression of Wealth in action, as well as how it has improved the lives of the many families we work with and how it can help you.

What's unique to baby boomers is that, in planning their legacy, part of that legacy is affording a strong education to their children and grandchildren. The Progression of Wealth provides this education. By modeling prudent financial choices for your children, they, too, will develop a solid appreciation for why planning is crucial—and the ability to create a plan for their own lives.

Anybody who has dreamed about financial independence but can't seem to move forward on the path to achieve it can benefit from reading this book. The only thing that stands between you and your dreams is the commitment to a process that will lead you there. The Progression of Wealth is that process, and this book is your guide.

CHAPTER 2

Maintaining Your Lifestyle, Not Just Your Life

We spend a majority of our life working toward retirement. In fact, so much of our time is spent working, working, working that when we finally reach retirement, the transition can be alarming.

If you haven't planned for retirement, the experience can be a lot like jumping into a pool filled with freezing water. The prospect is downright nerve-racking because you know the shock of hitting that frigid water just might keep you from floating back up to the surface.

Even if you *have* planned and saved, transitioning into retirement can be frightening, especially considering that few take the time to strategize life after work. And when we say "life," we're really talking about "lifestyle." That's an important distinction that many people inadvertently overlook.

How do you picture your lifestyle after retirement? Do you see yourself relaxing at that new vacation home, running your first 5K, and working in your newly landscaped backyard? Or do you see it as a time to sell the house, cancel that club membership, and cut out nights at your favorite restaurant?

The common view is that retirement is a time of drastic change. And in many regards, it is. Retirement incites a huge shift in identity, and also in your day-to-day life. But there is one aspect that should stay exactly the same: your lifestyle.

In other words, retirement is not a time to drastically change your lifestyle.

Retirement is a time to live out your well-earned dreams. You've worked long and hard to reach this point in your life, and at the very least, you deserve the security of being able to maintain your status of living into the next phase.

However, because retirement is a time when you are no longer saving, but rather, drawing from your savings, there's a common misconception that in order to survive, you must cut back.

That's where we differ from many other financial planners and advisors. For us, the key to survival is not cutting back, restricting your lifestyle, or "making do with less." The key is stability and comfort to maintain your lifestyle.

Creating Stability

Stability may sound like a simple solution—and it is—but the process of creating it is somewhat more complex. When you're planning for retirement, it's difficult to determine what you may have in the future and what your income streams will be. Furthermore, inflation will inevitably have an effect on your assets, which will also change the way your retirement plan pans out.

But that shouldn't make you feel helpless. On the contrary, that's all the more reason why it's crucial that you plan well. As we discussed in Chapter 1, a comprehensive retirement plan takes into account that we live in an uncertain world, and protects you against seen *and* unforeseen possibilities. An unhappy retirement does not happen because you planned and the world changed. An unhappy retirement happens when you do not plan at all.

So the first step in creating stability is simply having a plan.

At this point, you might be throwing your hands up, saying, "Hey, don't look at me! I have a plan. I met with an advisor ten years ago, and I've diligently stuck with it."

If this is the case, we commend you for taking charge of your future. However, this reveals another misconception about retirement planning. Many consider retirement planning a one-time deal, rather than an ongoing process. Like any financial plan, retirement is a living, breathing entity that requires reassessment and adaptations.

That's the second step in creating stability: realizing that a retirement plan is going to evolve, much like you will. Just because you're retired doesn't mean you've stopped growing or learning. In some ways, you have whole new windows of opportunity opened to you—and your retirement plan should mirror that same openness.

Financial plans are funny things. They change and mutate drastically. The plan that seemed so stable ten years ago could fail to support you in the evolving economy fifteen years in the future. The same strategies that made someone a millionaire ten years ago could make him dirt poor today.

Transitioning into retirement calls for a transition in the way you manage your assets and the financial goals you have in place. But figuring out where to go after forming your goals can be downright dizzying.

It's an interesting paradox: To create stability, you have to create a plan that can—and probably will—change. You also have to know what you value and the goals you'd like to achieve. This requires a desire to both maintain the lifestyle you're accustomed to while *simultaneously* making allowances for new passions you'll discover, new trips you'll take, and a shifting focus to issues of legacy and what you'll leave behind.

That's a lot to keep in mind! So how exactly do you strike the right balance? How do you do all of these things while also ensuring that your money can support you through them?

That's where the experts come in.

How Good Advisors Can Help

It is crucial to have a trusted advisor to guide you through your preparations for retirement. There are so many moving parts and strategies to consider. Managing your estate is a full-time job, which is why having a team of experts on hand can go a long way toward giving you ultimate peace of mind.

A financial advisor should build a life-long relationship with you based on clarity and insight about your finances. When considering potential advisors, always go with the financial advisor who has your best interests in mind, not just one concerned with commissions. Look to their client relationships. How are their client-retention rates? What referrals do they have? Are they fiduciaries?

The way in which your financial advisor works with you is as important as the plan he or she prepares. Your financial plan determines the lifestyle you can sustain. It enables you to cover any expenses that may arise, as well as to enjoy the things you love. If you feel your current advisor isn't hearing you when you talk about what is most important to you, it's probably time to find a new advisor.

Given the importance of your financial health, you can see why it is critical that you put as much trust into your relationship with your financial advisor as you would in your relationship with your doctor, counselor, pastor, or therapist. You wouldn't continue seeing a doctor who was writing prescriptions only to make money from pharmaceutical kickbacks, would you? Then why would you allow a financial advisor to do the same?

We started our firm because we were bothered by how traditional financial-services companies treat their clients. Rather than putting their clients' interests first, these companies are often focused on selling products in order to improve their own financial results, not necessarily their clients' financial standing.

Because of the limited scope of products these firms offer, they rarely learn about the client's retirement goals or take the complete view needed to manage clients' wealth for retirement. And, as a result, they can seriously hurt their clients' chances of enjoying the kind of retirement they've always dreamed about.

Most financial-services companies avoid a comprehensive planning process that addresses all aspects of wealth management. They choose, instead, to sell investment products based on fear and greed. Why? Because it is easier and more lucrative and requires a lot less work on their part. Comprehensive planning is labor intensive and requires detailed attention from a qualified professional who understands the interplay between investments, taxes, estate planning, insurance, and your goals.

Many people who call themselves financial advisors are merely salespeople focused on earning high-commission incomes. And that's simply unacceptable. Too many good, hardworking men and women have been hurt already—their finances decimated—because their advisor didn't have their best interest at heart.

In contrast, our process is advice-driven and centered on finding solutions that address all disciplines specified in the financial-planning process outlined by the Certified Financial Planner Board of Standards, the governing body of the Certified Financial Planner profession. Only from decades of experience in working with clients to plan their financial goals throughout all stages of life were we able to develop our process of securing financial independence. And this process has been proven to guide our clients toward achieving their goals, both financial and non-financial, in retirement. It is this exact same process that we're going to share with you.

In these pages, we will be unfolding our unique process, step by step. By the end of the book, you'll know all of the ingredients that go into a successful retirement, which will only empower you to find a trusted advisor to guide you through The Progression of Wealth. The right advisor can make all the difference in unlocking the retirement of your dreams.

Follow us to the next chapter as we introduce you to our tried-and-true method of creating financial security, stability, and a Blueprint for the life you've always wanted—the life you deserve.

CHAPTER 3

The Progression of Wealth

As principals of Meridian Wealth Partners, we've encountered a wide variety of financial situations with people from all walks of life. We've helped families plan for their parents' long-term care, ensuring their mom and dad were well cared for as they aged. We've seen couples who were doubtful about their ability to send their children to college not only live out their retirement dreams of ensuring their children were educated, but to actually support their grandchildren in *their* educational pursuits. We've helped business owners and corporations put together packages that provide security and benefits to their employees so that they can rest easy, knowing everyone is cared for.

Regardless of where our clients came from or what kind of situation they found themselves in, they were all searching for the same thing: financial independence.

Because we are the type of guys who measure and analyze everything, we tracked our process with our clients and closely observed the strategies we employed to help them achieve financial independence. Over time, we began to notice a pattern—one that was independent of the career, background, or financial portfolio of the client. From that pattern we were able to develop a process that works time and again, for people of all backgrounds seeking a variety of financial goals.

That process, as you know, became The Progression of Wealth, and has since enabled hundreds of families to achieve their dreams of financial independence, giving them the security and resources to live out their retirement dreams. Thanks to The Progression of Wealth, they will enter into retirement with the ability to support themselves and live the life they envisioned, rather than the one they were forced to live due to poor planning.

We created The Progression of Wealth in order to provide a personal process to help our clients meet their financial goals. At the time of its creation, no other firm was using a time-tested process for their services. As a result, The Progression of Wealth was not only effective; it was revolutionary.

The Simple Things in Life

We believe that our success as a financial-advising firm is not solely reliant on our knowledge and professional credentials. We believe that we were able to create a truly unique process—a proven way of understanding our clients' unique goals—all because we started in the same place in which we find many of our clients the moment they walk through our door: seeking security and simplicity.

Like the clients we serve, we value security and the ability to provide for our families. We enjoy the simple things in life. When Jay isn't guiding clients toward achieving their financial dreams, he enjoys a casual round of golf, traveling with his wife, and boating on the Atlantic with his three kids and grandchildren.

Brian also leads a busy family life with his wife and two kids. On his off-hours, Brian serves as Cub Master of his son's Scout pack. As a family, they like to spend their free time in the great outdoors—camping, hiking, and taking in the beautiful East Coast terrain.

Like every client we serve, we desire the security and reassurance that our futures are planned and cared for. We want to know that our children and loved ones will be taken care of. Brian wants to ensure that his children will have the opportunity to attend the college of their choice, debt-free.

We have studied and practiced the rigors of financial planning, sure. We would not be where we are today if we hadn't. But we were able to develop this process because our goals and our clients' goals are one and the same: financial independence.

The Fragmented-Finances Trap

You didn't make this money overnight. You earned it through hard work and prolonged effort, and you need a plan to match the amount of care you put forth to create it. You need a system and professional resources to guide you through each step of the process in order to ensure that you can reach your retirement goals. Unfortunately, many people we work with come to us because they find themselves in the "Fragmented-Finances Trap." It happens more often than you can imagine. People fragment their finances by dealing with multiple brokers, banks, and other financial institutions, thinking they are spreading their risk. Or, they have a financial advisor who is more interested in selling investments than in protecting his clients' money.

In either case, this results in very little diversification and increases complexity. However, there is a solution. The sure-fire way to avoid the Fragmented-Finances Trap is by choosing that trusted expert who has your best interests at heart to inventory your accounts and what investments are held in them. Your advisor can then organize all your assets to provide clarity about the entirety of your financial holdings and simplicity in managing and monitoring your assets. It's simple, easy, and—most importantly—effective.

Investments that are likely to result in capital gains are usually placed in taxable accounts wherever possible, while income-oriented investments are generally placed in tax-deferred accounts. In addition, by examining your total portfolio, rather than viewing accounts as separate silos, you can ensure that you are properly diversified.

Performance reporting, tax management, and analytics are all accomplished more easily once a single trusted advisor is overseeing your assets. And it's all covered in The Progression of Wealth process, along with other detailed steps. After all, we designed these steps to ensure that you have all your bases covered.

The Plan in Action

At this point you're probably wondering, *what exactly is the process?* The process includes seven steps, each one focusing on the major components to a secure financial plan. We'll give you a synopsis of each step below, and then go on to expand on each section in the following chapters. By the end of the process, you'll have a clear picture of what you can do to create stability for yourself and your family in retirement.

1: Blueprint

An architect draws a Blueprint so that he can ensure the structure is strong enough to endure the elements, weather the storms, and stand the test of time. The Blueprint step serves the same purpose for your life. At this stage, we work on understanding the areas of your life where you may or may not be satisfied and begin organizing your financial matters to help you feel more secure about retirement. We also start to look at ways you can use your money to lead a more fulfilling life.

The purpose of this step is to help you determine what your goals are, the amount of money that will be needed to accomplish these goals, the opportunities that you may look forward to, the strengths you have to help you achieve these goals, and the risks that may block you from achieving them.

2: Foundation

Once the Blueprint is drawn up, the foundation can be laid. The Foundation step is about having a clear vision of what you want to achieve and confidence in knowing you are on track to creating financial comfort.

A good foundation is created by having the fundamentals in place. Fundamentals include having a clear vision of your goals and life transitions; a savings goal that is realistic and appropriate, given your aspirations; and assets and liabilities structured appropriately to help you achieve maximum financial comfort.

3: Independence

Independence is the ability to do what you want, when you want, all of the time. It is achieved when you have clarified your true values, have a vision of your ideal life, and have the foundation and long-term plan in place that enables you to achieve fulfillment. In this section, we'll discuss how your Blueprint and Foundation can enable you to achieve independence for yourself and for your family.

4: Investments

At this stage, it's time to evaluate your investment portfolio to determine whether your asset allocation is appropriate for the return needed to meet your goals. In addition, the risk inherent in your portfolio should be evaluated and discussed to ensure you are comfortable with the amount of risk being taken.

The goal of Investments is to optimize the return needed for you to meet your goals while taking the least amount of risk. At our firm, we create an asset allocation specifically tailored to you and your goals. Investments are managed in a fiduciary capacity, which simply means our firm is held to the highest level of standards by law to act in your best interests. We analyze and allocate investments with proven academic research and the best tools available. Finally, we ensure you have a great investment experience.

5: Protection

Protection is all about controlling risks according to a plan—and having a contingency plan when things don't go exactly as expected. Here, education and clarity mean you can live your life without unnecessary worry.

At this stage, it's time to make a comprehensive evaluation of all the risks that threaten you and your wealth. This ensures that you, your family, and your assets are protected. Your risk-management philosophy will be developed, and your current insurance, evaluated to determine if you have the right coverage and plans in place, or if there are gaps in coverage.

6: Legacy

Together, we design a wealth transition plan that minimizes taxes and maximizes benefit. Ultimately, we implement a plan that will relieve your surviving spouse and children of unnecessary stress and worry. This stage helps you structure your wealth to ensure that your loved ones are provided for and that your wealth passes to your family and/or favorite charities efficiently and effectively, while you're paying the least amount of taxes possible within the boundaries of the law.

We'll also discuss the Loved Ones' Letter™, a document that instructs your family and friends on exactly whom to contact in case of an emergency and includes a comprehensive list of all your assets, liabilities, insurance policies, trust documents, and wills. The Loved Ones' Letter provides peace of mind for the family member who is not primarily responsible for the personal finances—a huge and lasting gift.

7: Renewal

Renewal is an ongoing conversation. The Progression of Wealth is not linear, with a start and finish. As your life changes, so do your aspirations and constraints. In annual meetings, your goals and progress are reviewed. Your level of satisfaction drives the process. In this step, we will discuss what you can do to ensure your plan continues to work for you.

The Time to Start Is Now

Once you have completed The Progression of Wealth process, you will have accelerated your progress toward financial independence and retirement. You will have a clear vision of your future and a plan to achieve it.

In addition, you will be able to save more money, because your assets will be properly allocated, structured, and protected. Your investment portfolio will be optimized to maximize your return and minimize your risk. You will have a comprehensive risk management and estate plan, you will have reduced your taxes, and you will have secured your financial comfort. You will also have put an entire framework in place to ensure that your loved ones can act efficiently and effectively in case of illness or death. We can't possibly overstate what an incredible gift this is for the people you love.

Most importantly, once you have completed The Progression of Wealth, you will be able to continue to enjoy your lifestyle while protecting your family and achieving your personal and financial goals. It's as simple as that.

So let's take the first step in your Progression of Wealth. It's time to sit down and draw up the Blueprint for your successful retirement.

CHAPTER 4

Drawing the Blueprint for Your Financial Future

The first step to securing your financial future is to determine where you are today and where you want to go next. In order to do this, we will examine what your goals are, the amount of money you will need to accomplish these goals, the opportunities that you may look forward to in life, the strengths you have to help you achieve these goals, and the risk that you feel is involved in making this process happen.

So roll up your sleeves and let's get to work. It's time to draw up your Blueprint™.

The Progression of Wealth Blueprint will help you clarify your goals in five major areas:

1. Helping and protecting your family
2. Enjoying and protecting your lifestyle
3. Planning ahead
4. Building a legacy
5. Creating financial comfort

When you first meet with your advisor, establishing the Blueprint is like going on a first date; we're getting to know each another and deciding if we are a good fit. But unlike a first date, this is no time to worry about making a good impression or saying the wrong thing. Lay it all out on the table and tell your advisor everything—about where you came from, what you value, and what you hope to achieve in the future. Once we get a sense of who you are, we can begin to draw up your financial framework to support all of the unique things that you value in life.

Compiling your Blueprint is not all about money and finances. After all, your Progression of Wealth plan is comprehensive. It's the foundation that supports all of the things that fill your life—the hobbies, travel plans, home renovations, and dreams of sending your kids to college. Your personal dreams and values are just as important as your budget, investments, and retirement accounts. We look at all of this information to find out where you want to be. This process helps us uncover the resources we'll be working with in order to get you there.

So where do we begin? On a first date, you usually start with a drink or a movie and then make your way to dinner (assuming all goes well). In the Blueprint stage, however, it all begins with a deck of cards. And no, we're not talking about tarot cards or even a normal deck with hearts, diamonds, clubs, and spades. We have created a very different and specialized deck of cards, carefully crafted from decades of experience in helping our clients articulate exactly what they want and need.

The Story of Your Financial Future Is in the Cards

The deck of cards we deal consists of fifty-two distinct goals that could possibly be in your future. It covers far-ranging dreams and desires, both tangible and intangible, everything from "buying a boat" to "providing for long-term care." The deck is just a starting point for generating the big picture of your financial future.

Along with anyone else involved in the planning process, we go through the cards to decide which things are important to you over the next five years, the next ten years, and the next twenty.

Which are immediate goals?

Which are future goals?

Of course, there may be additional goals that you will discover during the process; be sure to add those too. These cards are simply a starting point.

After going through the cards, it's time to plot your goals on The Progression of Wealth Blueprint. Most likely, you have more than a few cards in your deck. Life is full of surprises, needs, and desires, and these are all revealed in your cards, most likely in the form of a heaping pile. Our focus is to narrow these goals that you and your spouse have planned out. From the pile of cards, you must select the top ten that are most important to you.

These ten cards represent the most immediate goals of the deck. Maybe you need to provide medical assistance for an aging parent. Maybe you need some much-needed improvements on the house. Or maybe you plan to retire in the next five years. These are the cards that go into the top ten so that we can prioritize your financial plan around these goals. We want to make sure you have the resources to support these crucial ten things. Of course, in an ideal situation, you'll have plenty left over afterward, but we want to make sure those ten goals are covered no matter what.

What's Your Wake-up Call?

But wait—how do you choose just ten? How do you know which goals are the best investment? Which goals can wait for later? If there are fifty, or even twenty things that are important to you, choosing ten is hard!

As we mentioned earlier, your financial plan is fluid and ever changing. You may feel anxiety when it comes to choosing only ten—and the ten most important, no less— but know that once these goals are reached, you will have the freedom to move on to others, at each stage, feeling more secure because you have an adaptable plan to help you attain and sustain financial independence.

If you're having trouble narrowing down your goals, it's time to have what we call the "waking up at two o'clock in the morning" talk. You know those things that rouse you from sleep in the middle of the night and nag at you until the sun comes up? These are the major risks you are facing that you must try to manage to an acceptable degree. Although these risks are anxiety inducing, they are powerful tools for planning your Blueprint. By determining what it is that worries you the most, you can devise a plan to manage, if not negate, that risk.

The opposite of risk is opportunity. Not all the thoughts that wake you up at two o'clock in the morning are scary; they could also include the stuff about which you are delighted and thrilled.

- What are the things that wake you up at night because you're so excited, you can't stop thinking about them?

- What are the dreams that make your heart pound because they are such great opportunities, you just can't wait to take advantage of them?
- What are the things you've been waiting your whole life to accomplish, which you'll finally have the time and ability to do in retirement?

All of these also go to the top of the list. The goals you are most excited about, naturally, are the ones you will be most successful in attaining. The power of positive thinking can put you on the fast track to realizing your goals.

The purpose of this exercise is to bring insight into the cards in your deck. By doing this, you'll clarify your goals around these opportunities, and mitigate the risk through sound financial-planning strategies. So when it comes to choosing your top ten, first consider: What is your two o'clock in the morning wake-up call?

A Goal by Any Measure

Once you've agreed upon the top ten most important goals, it's time to set a deadline for those goals. After all, a goal has to be measurable, and the best way to track progress and gauge results is to assign a date to each goal. An added bonus is that these deadlines provide a pathway that will show you how we'll get the job done. Make it your challenge and adventure to stick to The Progression of Wealth and meet your deadline.

What goes into a deadline?

Quite simply, we assign the amount needed for your goal and estimate how long it will reasonably take you to get there.

For example, let's say you are thinking about retirement. You've put in decades of hard work, moved up the ladder, and really left your mark on your industry. Now it's time to relax and enjoy the fruits of your labor—but you're not quite ready. You figure you can last another five years at the office, and in our Blueprint process, you've determined that you need a minimum amount of money each year to live comfortably.

You know what you want; you know how much you need—now what? Back to the Blueprint. That goal of retirement with a minimum figure each year in five years' time all goes into the Blueprint grid. From there, we can structure your Progression of Wealth to accommodate this goal and deadline.

Does that sound overwhelming? No fear! Our clients often find Blueprint planning to be a really fun, enlightening, and stress-relieving exercise. Both you and your spouse are working together to decide which goals are the most important, which goals you'd like to achieve together, and which goals to work on individually.

Most of our clients express extreme satisfaction once they are finally laying out their plans and dreams so clearly and powerfully; it generates a lot of excitement for them. They enjoy the feeling that, at long last, they are actually moving toward the future with a tangible plan in place. Not only that; they are actually *designing* their future, taking an active part in co-creating their dreams.

This is the beginning of maximum peace of mind for you and your loved ones, and the launching pad for the life you have always wanted to live.

Now that you're beginning to see your goals laid out in front of you, you can take heart in the fact that you are one step closer to the financial future you desire. And because you've included us in this partnership, we will all work together to help you achieve these goals.

The last part of mapping out your Blueprint is evaluating personal satisfaction, or what you need in order to feel like you've achieved your goal. You've listed your top ten goals and determined the amount you'll need, as well as the deadline to be met, so now we dust off our crystal ball and peer into the future.

If we check in with you three years from today, what would have to happen with your financial plan in order for you to be satisfied? You may not know *exactly* how you'll feel in three years, but most people have a pretty good idea what would need to happen for them to feel satisfied and secure.

How far along toward your goals do you want to be in three years' time? What do you want your financial outlook to be like? Your lifestyle? One helpful exercise can be to imagine and actually map out a typical "day in the life" three years from now. In what ways is it the same as a day in your life today? In what ways is it different?

Evaluating personal satisfaction is another step in assessing your goals, assuring that your expectations are in alignment. Once your goals are properly aligned with your expectations, you can move along confidently, knowing that you are indeed achieving what you set out to do.

And there you have it: the beginning of a beautiful financial future, also known as your Blueprint. The Blueprint will serve as a clear guide to The Progression of Wealth financial plan that we will build upon in the following chapters. In fact, the Blueprint will become the backbone of every decision you'll make going forward.

Once you've completed the Blueprint, you will feel a sense of clarity about your goals and the ways you will reach them. You will truly understand the partnership that you and your spouse have formed using The Progression of Wealth to achieve your goals. Even better, you will begin to enjoy the feelings that come from having financial comfort. You will feel more secure about retirement, your future, and your ability to continue to enjoy your lifestyle. You will also rest easy in the knowledge that you'll be able to help your children in the future and leave a legacy behind. This will add confidence to how you choose to use your money *today*, paving the way for a more fulfilling life.

The Blueprint in Practice

Now that you know the fundamentals of creating your financial Blueprint, it's time to try it out for yourself. Below, you'll find our step-by-step guide to drawing up your Blueprint. Take time with your partner to consider the questions. Fill in the blanks with your dreams and goals, and keep these with you as we move along to the advanced stages of The Progression of Wealth.

What is important to you?

1. Taking Care of Family

_____

_____

_____

2. Enjoying Your Lifestyle

_____

_____

_____

3. Planning for the Future

_____

_____

_____

4. Building a Legacy

_____

_____

_____

5. Financial Comfort

_____

_____

_____

It's All in the Cards

Now that the wheels are turning in terms of what is most important to you, channel that into the card game. Scan the list below. These are the fifty-two items we affix to our fifty-two cards, and they correspond to the dreams, fears, and desires most commonly expressed by our clients. They aren't all "goals"; some of them are things that could happen in the future, events or crises for which you may want to be prepared.

Which of these fifty-two speak to you? As you identify the pieces that fit together to create your unique financial picture, write each one down on a card. Expand on your big-picture dreams and fears—the more detail the better, since the more clearly you can see your dream, the better equipped you will be to attain it. The same goes for your fears: The more clearly you can envision them, the better you can prepare for the worst (and hope for the best).

What are some of your goals, challenges, and concerns that *aren't* on the list? Make sure to include those in your deck too. It's never one-size-fits-all, so don't rush or feel like you have to accept every single one you see here. We encourage you to take time to consider all the wonderfully unique things you want to accomplish in the years to come, and all the scary stuff that wakes you up in a cold sweat in the middle of the night. The more detailed your deck, the fuller a picture you will draw of your retirement, and the better we will be able to assist you in facing anything and everything that comes your way.

Life Goals/Potential Challenges

1. Sell a home
2. Relocate
3. Reevaluate investment philosophy
4. Debt concerns
5. Receive inheritance or financial windfall
6. Change in marital status
7. Child with special needs
8. Child going to college
9. Child getting married
10. Family special event (bat/bar mitzvah, anniversary party, special trip)
11. Helping and/or gifting to grandchildren
12. Concern about aging parents

13. Provide for long-term care (parent, spouse/partner, or self)
14. Medical insurance
15. Helping or gifting to children
16. Develop an estate plan
17. Address an important health issue
18. Attend a personal-development event
19. Begin a new hobby
20. Begin an exercise program
21. Develop or master a skill
22. Go back to school to earn a degree or certification
23. Learn a new language
24. Take art/music/dance lessons
25. Assist a family member with a home purchase
26. Assist a family member with income needs
27. Help parents
28. Fund education expenses for a family member
29. Miscellaneous purchase for a family member
30. Provide long-term care for a family member
31. Purchase an automobile
32. Send a family member on a trip
33. Acquire or purchase a business
34. Change a career path
35. Develop a phased retirement plan
36. Learn new skills by receiving advanced training or education

37. Retirement
38. Take a sabbatical or leave of absence
39. Go away on a hobby-related trip
40. Go on a family vacation
41. Go on a trip
42. Go on an adventure tour
43. Live in another country
44. Purchase a family vacation home
45. Purchase a motor home
46. Purchase a boat
47. Major purchase
48. Create or fund a foundation
49. Include charities in my estate plan
50. Make ongoing contributions to specific charities
51. Make home improvements
52. Not be a burden on children

The Final Cut

You know the drill. Now that you've got the cards that are important to you, it's time to decide which ten cards make the final cut. Again, don't worry about "sacrificing" goals in order to choose the top ten. As you move closer to your goals, you will make room to include others. For now, your job is simple: Just narrow it down!

Once you choose your top ten, assign a "deadline" or "due date" and determine what resources each one will require.

How much do you need in order to meet that goal or prepare for that potential challenge? And what's a reasonable time frame in which you can meet that goal? Use the chart below to map out your Blueprint in a clear, actionable way.

My Financial Blueprint: Top Ten Goals

	Goals	Date	Amount
1			
2			
3			
4			
5			
6			
7			
8			
9			
10			

By honing in on what is most important to you, you have hopefully gained confidence and clarity about your financial goals, and now that you have your Blueprint, it's time to make them happen.

45

In the next chapter, we'll use the Blueprint and the knowledge we've surfaced so far to build and fortify your financial foundation. The Blueprint is just the first step; now that we have uncovered the resources we're working with, we can outline the actions we recommend.

No good architect packs up shop after simply writing the plans. Our ultimate goal is to build you a whole house—one that is beautiful and strong and which will offer you security and comfort for as long as you need it. In the next chapter, we'll pour the foundation of that very house.

C H A P T E R   5

Setting the Foundation to Build Toward Your Goals

The definition of foundation is "the basis on which a thing stands, is founded, or is supported." Laying the foundation is the first step after creating the Blueprint, and it has to be strong enough to support the structure that is built on top of it. Any holes or structural weaknesses, and the building could come crashing down.

The same can be said of your financial plan.

In the last chapter, you assessed your goals and needs and wrote them up in the Blueprint. You now understand what you *want* your future to look like, but you've yet to formulate *how* you will achieve it.

The Foundation is the first step in making your goals a reality. We call this stage of The Progression of Wealth the "Foundation" because it is at this point that we evaluate the very basis of your financial plan.

Building your Foundation means developing a clear sense of the resources, needs, and goals that are specific to you. It also means that you have the fundamentals in place.

Fundamentals include:
- A clear vision of your goals and life transitions
- A savings goal that is realistic and appropriate, given your aspirations
- Assets and liabilities structured appropriately to help you achieve financial comfort

To set foot on the ladder of financial freedom and begin The Progression of Wealth, you have to know where you stand and how much farther you will need to climb to reach your destination.

It doesn't take a degree in finance to know that reaching your financial goals comes down to one thing: money.

You know that what you do with your money will determine whether or not you will achieve the retirement of your dreams, but perhaps you don't know where it goes, or where to put it.

We have found that, while many people are good at making money, they don't always have a feel for their budget. And by budget, we're referring to the month-to-month cash-flow base throughout the year. The bills and mortgage are taken care of, but where does the rest of it go?

The most common excuse we hear from people who put off saving for retirement is that there are simply too many things that need to be taken care of *now*.

The bathroom needs to be redone *now*.

We need to replace the SUV *now*.

Our son is going to college *now*.

The list goes on and on and on. These needs and desires are often prioritized because they produce an immediate result, whereas investing and saving money relies upon time to bloom and grow. And so saving for retirement gets pushed onto the back burner.

But what if I told you that you can plan for retirement, and plan for your needs—both expected and unexpected—that may arise in the immediate future?

On a savings plan, you can fulfill all of your needs. You can redo the bathroom, extend the kitchen, and buy the new car and vacation house on the beach. But you can only do it—that's right—with a plan. A good savings plan dictates that money goes into savings first, and on a consistent basis.

Oftentimes, people believe having a savings plan means that they can kiss their cash goodbye, but that's simply not the case. We find that most of our clients are surprised by how well their savings plan works for them, and that they can, and do, enjoy all of the things they were doing before.

Life in the present doesn't change; it's your life in the future that transforms—and for the better.

Building the Foundation

You may be asking yourself, *Where can I save?*

And more importantly, *Where should it go?*

Most people don't have a good feel for their budget, and as a result, money that could be growing your future is underutilized, leaving dollars on the table.

So first things first: What's your cash flow?

Where is your money coming from each month?

Where is it going?

It's important to understand these factors so that you can see exactly what is required each month, and what can be spared. Of course, unexpected expenses may pop up over the course of the year, but as we mentioned, you can plan for that.

We have made this step in your Progression of Wealth easier for you with a handy tool. Following this chapter, we have provided a budget worksheet that will allow you to get a detailed view of your current financial profile.

Use this tool to determine where your monthly expenditures are going, and identify where you can save. Compare this to the figures that you will require in retirement. This is an important step that will come into play in the following chapter. For now, take time to consider your current habits and how those might play into your long-term goals.

Savings Priority List

Even if you're on board with saving to your full potential, you may not be certain of how best to utilize that money. The Savings Priority List will help you to identify the four main areas that will contribute to your financial plan.

When you're dealing with a household that includes children, mortgages, cars, investments, and more, it can seem nearly impossible to sift through all of the data to see where the money is going, and what you should target first. This list will narrow it down for you.

Priority #1: Paying Down Bad Debt First

Bad debt is defined as high-interest-rate debt that has no tax benefits. Typically, that covers anything that is above 6% interest rate, including credit card debt and most often student loan debt. If you're carrying credit card debt at 10% and above, then before you start saving anywhere, pay down that debt.

Priority #2: Employer-Sponsored Retirement Plan

This is our next favorite place to save. Absolutely take advantage of any match your employer is offering. If the company is matching 3%, but you have to put 6% in, then make sure you at least capture the "free money."

What we find most often is that one spouse is saving in their plan and the other is not because he or she believes the other spouse is taking care of that. As a result, you may be losing some employer-matching dollars. Capitalize on anything that is available to you through your company. Put the maximum amount allowed by law into the 401K plan; otherwise, it's a wasted opportunity.

Priority #3: Goal-Based Funding

This takes into consideration things like education for your kids. If you have kids, and college education is a goal, then look to 529 tax-advantage savings plans for your children's future.

Priority #4: Taxable Savings

Once you have exhausted all of your tax advantage savings, the rest of your savings we call "taxable savings" because there are no benefits to saving it. Later on we'll discuss how you can maximize on the earning potential of these savings.

It's Never Too Soon to Sock It Away

Trying to plan as catch-up when it comes to saving for retirement puts a lot of unnecessary pressure and risk on you. The longer you have your money invested, the more potential you have for growing your wealth—hands down. It's easy to put it off for more present-day desires, but know that with a proper plan, you will be able to handle unexpected expenses as well as achieve your personal goals.

Instead of dreaming about all of the improvements you'd like to make, the trips you'd like to take, and other wonderful things, make it a reality. A financial plan is the only tool that can make those dreams a reality by examining what you need in order to achieve them. With the help of our budgeting tool, in addition to the Savings Priority List, you now know how your plan may begin to take form. And you know that to succeed and retire with financial comfort, you have to start with the basics.

Taking stock of your everyday household finances and understanding your real financial picture are the actions that make up the solid foundation from which your retirement plan begins. Now that you have a comprehensive view of your goals and current portfolio, it's time to link the two together. Follow along to the next phase of your Progression of Wealth toward Financial Independence.

Name(s): _____   **Date:** _____

Income:

	You	Spouse/Partner
Annual Salary/Earned Income		
Estimated Annual Bonus		
Other Income (gifts, trust, rental income, money owed to you, etc.)		
Total Income		

Assets:

	You	Spouse/Partner	Joint
Checking/Savings Accounts			
Money Market/CDs/Other Cash Reserves (describe)			
401ks			
IRAs			
Taxable Investment Accounts (mutual funds, stocks, etc)			
Home Value			
2nd Home Value			
Other (describe)			
Total Assets			

Debts/Liabilities:

	You	Spouse/Partner	Joint
Mortgage 1			
Mortgage 2			
Credit Cards			
Education Loans			
Auto Loans			
Other (describe)			
Total Debts/Liabilities			

Insurance and Estate Documents:

	You	Spouse/Partner
Life Insurance		
Disability Insurance		
Have Wills (indicate Yes or No)		

The Progression of Wealth

Meridian WEALTH PARTNERS.

Budget Data Gathering Worksheet

Personal and Family Expenses

Category	Monthly Budget Amount	
	Current	Retirement
Alimony		
Bank Charges		
Books/Magazines		
Business Expenses		
Care for Parent/Other		
Cash – Misc./ATM		
Cell Phone		
Charitable Donations		
Child Activities		
Child Allowance/Expense		
Child Care		
Child Support		
Child Tutor		
Clothing – Client(s)		
Clothing - Children		
Club Dues _____		
Credit Card Debt Pmt		
Dining Out		
Education/Tuition		
Entertainment		
Gifts		
Groceries		
Gym/Self Improvement		
Healthcare – Dental		
Healthcare – Medical		
Healthcare – Prescription		
Healthcare – Vision		
Hobbies _____		
Household Items		
Laundry/Dry Cleaning		
Personal Care		
Pet Care		
Public Transportation		
Recreation		
Student Loan Payment		
Vacation/Travel		
Other		

Personal Insurance Expenses

Category	Monthly Budget Amount	
	Current	Retirement
Disability for Client		
Disability for Spouse		
Life for Client		
Life for Spouse		
LTC for Client		
LTC for Spouse		
Medical for Client		
Medical for Spouse		
Umbrella Liability		
Other		

Taxes

Category	Monthly	Annual
Client Federal		
Client State		
Client Local (if applicable)		
Client FICA		
Client Medicare		
Spouse Federal		
Spouse State		
Spouse Local (if applicable)		
Spouse FICA		
Spouse Medicare		
Other		

Budget Data Gathering Worksheet

Home #1 Expenses

Description: _____

Category	Monthly Budget Amount	
	Current	Retirement
First Mortgage		
Second Mortgage		
Equity Line		
Real Estate Tax		
Rent		
Homeowner's Insurance		
Association Fees		
Electricity		
Gas/Oil		
Trash Pickup		
Water/Sewer		
Cable/Satellite TV		
Internet		
Telephone (land line)		
Lawn Care		
Maintenance - Major Repair		
Maintenance - Regular		
Furniture		
Household Help		
Other		

Vehicle #1 Expenses

Description: _____

Category	Monthly Budget Amount	
	Current	Retirement
Loan Payment		
Lease Payment		
Insurance		
Personal Property Tax		
Fuel		
Repairs/Maintenance		
Parking/Tolls		
Docking/Storage		
Other		

Vehicle #2 Expenses

Description: _____

Category	Monthly Budget Amount	
	Current	Retirement
Loan Payment		
Lease Payment		
Insurance		
Personal Property Tax		
Fuel		
Repairs/Maintenance		
Parking/Tolls		
Docking/Storage		
Other		

The
Progression
of Wealth

Budget Data Gathering Worksheet

Home #2 Expenses

Description: _____

Category	Monthly Budget Amount	
	Current	Alt1 / Retirement
First Mortgage		
Second Mortgage		
Equity Line		
Real Estate Tax		
Rent		
Homeowner's Insurance		
Association Fees		
Electricity		
Gas/Oil		
Trash Pickup		
Water/Sewer		
Cable/Satellite TV		
Internet		
Telephone (land line)		
Lawn Care		
Maintenance - Major Repair		
Maintenance - Regular		
Furniture		
Household Help		
Other		

Vehicle #3 Expenses

Description: _____

Category	Monthly Budget Amount	
	Current	Alt1 / Retirement
Loan Payment		
Lease Payment		
Insurance		
Personal Property Tax		
Fuel		
Repairs/Maintenance		
Parking/Tolls		
Docking/Storage		
Other		

Vehicle #4 Expenses

Description: _____

Category	Monthly Budget Amount	
	Current	Alt1 / Retirement
Loan Payment		
Lease Payment		
Insurance		
Personal Property Tax		
Fuel		
Repairs/Maintenance		
Parking/Tolls		
Docking/Storage		
Other		

CHAPTER 6

Declaring Your Financial Independence

Independence is the ability to do what you want, when you want, where you want, all the time. Independence is achieved when you have clarified your true values, have a vision of your ideal life, and have in place the foundation and long-term care plan that enable you to achieve a fulfilling life.

The path to independence is not always so clear. In fact, surprisingly, most successful executives and business owners who have achieved significant wealth lack confidence in their future. Typically, they don't have clear goals or a plan to achieve them. Their investments aren't organized, or they have the wrong insurance policies—maybe too much or not enough.

Perhaps their investment allocation won't allow them to achieve their goals. They're too risky or too conservative, or they may be taking on too much risk for the reward they may receive.

Or maybe they don't fully understand their company benefits and aren't taking full advantage of their plans, or they are relying too much on their company stock. They pay too much in taxes. Their wills are not complete or current. They do not have all of their beneficiaries named. They use many advisors, but the advisors are not being coordinated and do not work together.

For these reasons—and more—they are unnecessarily worried about their future and are not enjoying life as much as they could.

We call this living in the "Fragmented-Finances Trap."

In most of the cases, people find themselves in the Fragmented-Finances Trap not because they're poor money managers, but because they, like many others, have been led to believe in money myths that hurt, rather than help them.

Five Money Myths
That Fragment Your Finances

Myth #1: Any debt is bad debt.

Contrary to popular belief, not all bad debt is created equal. In fact, debt can be divided into two categories: good, and bad.

As we touched on in the previous chapter, credit card debt, certain leases or auto loans, personal loans—these all exist on the evil axis of bad debt. And like most things that are bad for us, in the beginning, they seem downright tempting. This debt is introduced to us with a low interest rate (aka, "teaser rate"), but once the introductory period is up, that interest rate increases. In effect, we end up paying for twice for one item. It all seems like a great deal to begin with, but no great deal exists in the land of bad debt.

So what could possibly constitute good debt?

In order to answer this question, ask yourself, *Is there a better opportunity to use the money elsewhere?*

In other words, is there an opportunity to invest that money that would give you a greater return than the interest rate of your debt? And this leads us to the following myth-buster:

Myth #2: Paying off mortgage early is good because you build up equity faster.

A mortgage tends to equate to good debt, especially in terms of the interest rate. Think about it: The average annual return for the stock market over the long term is around 8-to-12%. The average mortgage rate is usually half of that—or less.

Which presents the greater opportunity to earn more in the long run?

It seems counterintuitive, but remember that old maxim about time and money: It all pays off in the long run. And if that doesn't convince you, consider the fact that you get an income tax deduction for the mortgage interest that you do pay. The tax deduction cuts down even more on the mortgage borrowing rate, which equals more dollars in the long run, as that money spends more time invested in the market.

Myth #3: Investing in real estate, especially your house, always pays off.

People view their home as their most valuable asset—and indeed, it is. Your home will be the most valuable thing that you own, not just in terms of the money you put into it, but also in terms of the role it plays in your life. Your home is where you live, raise kids, celebrate holidays, entertain, and relax on your time off. But a retirement savings it *does not* make.

If you were to hold out for a strong market, and then move into a smaller home, then yes, you could view your home as an asset. However, we have found that's usually not the case. Most people leave their home for a larger, upgraded, and more costly home, which amounts to zero savings.

The best way to make your home work for you is to buy a house that you can afford. Leave real estate investments to the professionals.

Myth #4: You can pay for things today out of your salary and make up savings later through bonuses and pay raises.

We've written this before (OK, maybe more than a few times now), but it still bears repeating: Don't put off saving—not now, not ever!

You can find many reasons to use your savings for things you'd like to do today, but the truth is, your house will never be perfect, you'll always want a new car, and your retirement will never recover.

To go into more detail, when you put money into a long-term investment strategy, you should earn 7% on that money, and over time, your money could double every ten years. Compounding takes time, but when you continue to postpone your savings, you will lose your most valuable asset. So do yourself a favor: Prioritize your savings plan. Make contributions automatic and, even more important, hard to get to.

Myth #5: The stock market is too risky.

People tend to view investing in the stock market as they do a trip to Vegas: It's a gamble, and you're more likely to come out with a headache and sore belly than a fistful of money.

Let's dispel that myth right now. To do that, take a look at a few of the wealthiest people in the world, both past and present: Andrew Carnegie, Bill Gates, and Sir Richard Branson. What do you think they do with their earnings? *They invest them.*

They know that the best way to maintain wealth, and to beat inflation, is to let their money make more money in the market.

The key ingredients here? Time and diversification. A trusted money manager will help you put together an Investment Policy Statement that will address your goals, time horizon, and risk tolerance. While the stock market does involve risk, it is risk that pays off in the long run.

Stick to the Plan

You picked up this book for a variety of reasons. Maybe you wanted to make sure you're on track with your finances, or maybe you wanted to make sure your loved one is making sound decisions. Either way, you started reading because you have a concern. You are concerned about what the future might hold.

Up to this point, you have been addressing this concern by first going through the Blueprint stage, which helped you clarify your goals. From there, you entered the Foundation stage and developed a better understanding of your current financial outlook.

You are ready to use this information to create a plan that will allow you to bridge the gap between now and that future—one that is not uncertain, but rather, in accordance with your goals, wishes, and desires.

Now you will coordinate your goals and develop a strategy so that both your short-term and long-term goals are working together. Not only will they be working together, but also your short-term goals will be assisting your long-term goals in perfect harmony.

Think back to the Blueprint stage. In the Blueprint, we helped you create a vision of your future. Now in Independence, we create a plan to achieve this vision.

This is an important and collaborative step in the process. There is no set formula for computing what you need; rather, the plan depends on your unique needs. When we meet with clients at this step of the process, we take the information they gathered in the Foundation stage and input it into the Cash-Flow Optimizer.

The Cash-Flow Optimizer is a unique tool that helps you determine how much money you have to invest to reach your financial goals. It also serves as a budgeting tool that can help you adjust your plan if you are not saving enough.

Additionally, as you move into retirement, the Cash-Flow Optimizer serves as a tool to help you spend your wealth or give it away to your family or charities.

The beauty of the Optimizer is that it is a multipurpose tool to help you accomplish savings, budgeting, retirement income, and gifting.

In order to utilize the Cash-Flow Optimizer, you must first identify all of your sources of income and, using the tool we provide, identify your expenses. This is completed in the Foundation stage.

The Optimizer uses factors such as rates of inflation, investments, and personal goals to project out over the years and visualize how these values will play out.

We use the Optimizer to create charts that look first at the heaviest savings part of life, what we call "preretirement." This is the period that typically occurs between the ages of fifty-five and sixty-five, when one's children have finished college, left the house, and are beginning their careers. This is also the time when expenses may be reduced a bit. There is a greater ability to start saving tremendously for the next stage, which may be retirement or financial independence.

This chart is extended all the way into retirement years

and shows how much money will be available, according to the savings plan that is formulated in the present.

The Optimizer takes what you've learned from working on all the other stages, pulls it all together, and creates the expected outcome. It is broken down by time periods so that not only will you know whether you will achieve your goals, but you'll also have a benchmark to work with, and check against, each year to see if you're on track.

For example, Kevin and Cindy make a combined income of $350,000. They are both in their fifties and have two children who will soon be entering college. With the help of the budgeting and expenses tool, they determined that they have the ability to save $70,721 a year. But if only it were so simple! In addition to the desire to retire comfortably, they have goals for their busy family.

During the Blueprint stage, they determined that their most important goals are to:
- Redo the upstairs bathroom
- Save for both children's weddings
- Save for both children's educations
- Have enough to retire and live comfortably

With their financial information, including how much they bring in, how much they spend, and how much they've already invested, we were able to project whether they would be able to meet all of their goals. And if they weren't, we could advise where to allocate their assets to make their dreams a reality.

We highly recommend that you find a trusted advisor to walk you through how your own plan will play out over the course of your life. We have found that the biggest mistakes people make when it comes to their savings, aside from putting it off, is that they don't have a thorough understanding of their income and expenditures, and they overestimate their ability to save later on. This step frees you from that burden. You will be able to see, with precise accuracy, how your decisions now will affect you ten, twenty, and even fifty years into the future.

Once you complete the Financial Independence phase, you will know what your income is, what your expenses are, and what potential funds will go into your portfolio, and in the event of retirement, what funds will come out.

Still having trouble believing you can meet your savings goals?

Here's a word of advice: Cash doesn't lie.

Once you determine your ability to save, stick to that plan, even if it seems extreme. Once you start, one of two things will happen: Your bank account is going to go down too much because you're saving too much, or it's going to stay the same. I'm willing to bet that, with the help of these tools, you're not going to miss the money. In fact, you're going to love all of the extra work that your money will do for you.

How can you ensure that you'll have the ability to meet all of your goals, pay your living expenses, and not run out of money? You'll know because you'll have investments as security. In the next chapter, you will learn what kinds of investments can grant you that security.

CHAPTER 7

Financial Education Will Lead to Choosing the Right Investments

When it comes to your finances, the best way to grow your wealth and protect it is to invest it. The caveat, however, is that the formula only works if you have the *right* investment strategy.

The best proven method for making the right investment strategy relies upon sound decision-making based on academic research. Sounds easy enough, until you factor in the sheer volume of information and research available to the average consumer. You can find in-depth instructions on practically every subject, but just because you can read about the theory of relativity on Wikipedia, that doesn't make you a cosmologist.

The same logic applies to investing. Everyone has access to research and advice; the trick is to fully understand what matters in investing so that you can decide what is the right decision for you.

Good investing requires a good financial education, which a majority of Americans unfortunately don't have. In fact, if we had to assign a grade to a majority of clients when they first come to us, they would score between a C and an F on their financial education.

As harsh as that sounds, it illustrates the fundamental gap between security and fractured finances: an education. And that's just what we're going to give you in this chapter.

There are myriad options for financial instruments available to American investors today. It is our job to help you understand what you have and why certain recommendations will work for you.

Our commitment to financial education is unique to our wealth-management strategy, and how we see ourselves as a partner in your financial journey to independence. Once you are familiar with the vehicles that are available to you, you will be better equipped to lay out a detailed plan and choose specific financial investments that will allow you to reach your financial goals.

Armed with this knowledge, you will be empowered to make the right investments. So let's begin. We'll start with our philosophy of investing.

The Fundamentals

Our strategies are based upon two basic principles:

Principle #1: Markets work.

Capital markets are fairly priced and utilize all available information to determine investor expectations about publicly traded securities. There is a lot of confusion about how the market works, and what kind of returns people can expect from it. The stock market—which may have its ups and downs—is, in the long run, still the best method for growing your money, after inflation.

Principle #2: Portfolio structure determines performance.

The asset classes that comprise your portfolio and the risk level of those asset classes are responsible for most of the variable portfolio returns. In this sense, diversification is key. Having a comprehensive global asset allocation can neutralize the risk specific to individual securities, so that in the end, you win. At the same time, risk and return are related. The compensation for taking on increased levels of risk is the potential to earn greater returns, and vice versa.

Asset Allocation

While we're on the subject, let's take some time to expand your understanding of asset allocation.

The first step in designing your portfolio is asset allocation, and the first step in asset allocation is making a determination of how much to put into stocks versus how much to put into bonds and cash. This is a major decision that is determined by which time period of life you are currently in.

Want an idea of how important asset allocation really is? It affects a whopping 93% of investment success. The remaining 7% is the actual securities that are selected or managed.

Once you decide how much to put into stocks and bonds, the next determination is what sectors to use. Sectors in stocks could be the U.S. market versus the foreign market versus emerging markets. Sectors in bonds could be short-term bonds versus intermediate bonds versus long-term bonds, or even tax-free bonds versus taxable bonds.

These are all items to consider, and a trusted financial advisor will be able to guide you with these decisions. The important thing is that you understand the importance of asset allocation, and how it fluctuates according to how close you are to retirement.

Your Own Worst Enemy

At this stage in The Progression of Wealth, we would like to take a moment to quote the father of value investing himself, Benjamin Graham:

"The investor's chief problem—and even his worst enemy—is likely to be himself."

That's right: Most investors get into trouble not because of bad advice, but because of their own behavior. You could have the best counsel in the world, but if you ultimately act according to your own impulses, you will pay in the end.

Humans are not wired for disciplined investing. In a world of uncertainty, it's difficult to think ten, twenty, or even thirty years into the future when you're busy working on current goals. Not to mention, it's difficult to imagine what life will be like that far out. As a result, people lose sight of the big picture, investing gets placed on the back burner, and those potential long-term gains are cut in half.

Another aspect of lacking discipline is that many investors follow their emotions. When they hear a popular analyst on the news yell, "Sell! Sell!" they can't move their funds fast enough. Or if their neighbor boasts of their big wins with a particular stock, they are certain they will lose thousands of dollars unless they follow suit.

Reacting hurts performance. It all goes back to Benjamin Graham's wise words: The investor is his own worst enemy.

And that's why you need someone in your corner to take the emotional aspect out of investing and make the right decisions for your long-term goals.

Why is focusing on the long-term important? Because markets reward discipline. If there is one thing you should research on your own, it is the result of long-term investing. Type that into the Google search engine, and you will see the consistent gains from this practice and how it can work for you.

Beware Mental Errors

Emotional investing is flawed simply because it is based on false logic. We call this false logic "mental errors," and we've compiled a list of the beliefs people frequently reply upon to drastically change their investment approach:

1. *The market is going to crash.*
2. *I have a winning system for picking stocks.*
3. *My technical research confirms that this is a great stock to own.*
4. *I knew this stock was going up.*
5. *It was a bad idea, but I don't want to sell at a loss.*
6. *The trend looks good and should continue for a long time.*
7. *I work in that industry, so I know where it's going.*
8. *I wasn't wrong about that stock; I was just unlucky.*
9. *The market is too far up and I need to go to cash.*
10. *The market is too down and I need to go to cash.*

The next time you think about shuffling around your investments, check if any of these mental errors are in play—and then call your financial advisor.

Focus on What You Can Control

As difficult as it may seem, the best way you can help yourself is to focus on what you can control. Sometimes it is difficult to discern what exactly is within your power, so we'll spell it out for you. The following three factors will determine the likelihood of your financial plan's success, and the best news is that they are all within your control:

Taxes

Constant buying and selling creates taxable gains, as well as short-term capital gains. Depending on your tax bracket and the state you live in, these gains could deplete over 20-to-50% or more of your gains to taxes. This is where emotional buying and selling can really take a toll as those taxes add up. Your advisor can eliminate this threat by minimizing taxes and working them into your retirement plan to maximize your investments and avoid unnecessary taxes.

Risk Level

Pursuing a more aggressive investment strategy means increasing risk, which might be more appropriate for someone who is in the earlier stages of retirement planning. On the other hand, measures such as holding more bonds than stock decrease your risk, which appeals to those who are in retirement. You can't control how the market performs, but you can control the amount of risk you take on and find a comfortable arrangement that works for you, depending upon your stage in life.

Fees

"Fees" refers to any expenses you may pay your managers. By reducing those costs, you can substantially increase your returns. The one thing that you can't control all the time is return. No one can reliably forecast the market's direction, but by having an investment discipline and trimming excess costs, you will get—and keep—more of the market returns, and over time, these returns will be substantial.

Constructing Your Perfect Portfolio

Now that you understand the factors that play into smart investment practices, it's time to incorporate this knowledge.

In order to implement these strategies into your investment portfolio, first determine whether your asset allocations are appropriate for the returns needed to meet your goals and risk tolerance. It's important that the risk inherent in your portfolio is compared to that in your profile to ensure you are comfortable with the amount of risk being taken. The goal here is to optimize the return needed for you to meet your goals while taking the least amount of risk and paying the least amount of taxes. This is how asset allocation is designed to meet your needs.

Your job is to remember what you can control, while watching out for common mental errors that can sabotage your savings.

Your advisor's job is to compose a portfolio that balances stocks, bonds, and cash so that you and your loved ones will be covered in the future and realize the greatest results.

Once your portfolio is in place, you are well on your way to the retirement of your dreams. But there is still an important step to complete: protection. In the next chapter, we'll delve deeper into the subject of risk, and show you how you can protect your assets—and your family—by managing this crucial factor.

CHAPTER 8

Protecting Your Assets
and Your Family

Everything of value needs protection. You wouldn't put a million-dollar picture on display in a museum unless you knew the museum had a good security system to protect it from possible burglaries. You also wouldn't want to display it there unless you knew the museum was insured against any unforeseen emergencies like fires or floods.

That, in a nutshell, is what protection is about: having a security system to safeguard your valuables.

Establishing a financial plan, on the other hand, is like having your own treasure map leading you to the gold doubloons that will ensure your family's legacy. But without any kind of protection, there's no telling what obstacle could befall you and prevent you from reaching the buried treasure.

Regardless of the amount of planning one can do, the future is always uncertain. There are factors such as illness, accidents, and loss that simply cannot be predicted. You can plan your retirement down to the cent and still be subject to loss if you don't have a safety net. Similar to managing the amount of risk you take on, however, you can also manage your vulnerability to these unknown factors.

In this day and age, getting old is expensive; getting ill can be catastrophic. One of the most difficult decisions we face as we grow older is what to do when caring for a loved one, come what may. Nobody wants money to factor into the decisions he or she makes during times of serious strife or sorrow; however, ignoring the subject can equate to pressing the "self-destruct" button on one's estate.

The good news is that, with planning, there's no need to fear the future.

You can plan for anything life might throw your way and ensure your loved ones will get the care they need—no matter what.

You have now invested a good deal of time and interest in your unique financial plan. You've discovered what's most important to you and your partner when it comes to your finances and the future. You've established short- and long-term goals, and envisioned your ideal retirement.

Now that you have created your plan, it is time to address how you can protect these investments.

Being protected means controlling risk according to a plan, and having an alternative plan in place for when things don't go exactly as you'd imagined. It means being able to live your life without unnecessary worry or fear. In financial planning, your valuables are primarily your loved ones and your assets, and the trick here is to determine *what kind* of protection you really need. If you've learned anything by now, it's that there is no "one size fits all" plan when it comes to your financial needs; similarly, there is no uniform equation for the kind of protection you require. Determining your protection requires assessing your vulnerabilities.

The forces you are protecting against are the disabilities you may suffer, emergencies or property losses that are outside of your control, or even, God forbid, premature death. It's not a pleasant thought, but no financial plan is complete without taking care of these six essential threats:

1. Premature death of a spouse.
2. Disability of a wage earner.
3. Personal-liability lawsuit.
4. Property damage or loss.

5. Long-term sickness of a family member.

6. Taxes.

Life's most stressful situations can be avoided if you plan for them in advance. And in this chapter, we'll take a closer look at how you can face down these forces, one vulnerability at a time, and ensure you'll be protected.

Premature Death of a Spouse

Losing your partner is devastating; the last thing you want on top of that loss is to learn that you won't be able to sustain the life you once shared. A good life insurance policy will protect you and your partner from ever having to face down this uncertainty. However, selecting the policy that will work for you requires some thoughtful analysis.

First, you must conduct a "survivor-needs analysis." This determines the amount of life insurance you and your partner would require in the event he or she is on his or her own by plotting such things as future cash flows over both lifetimes. It also takes into account a present value calculation in today's money and how much each partner would need.

The survivor-needs analysis is based on a complex model, which a financial advisor can walk you through, but a basic rule of thumb is that in order to retire and educate a child through college, you need a minimum of $1 million in life insurance.

That may seem like a substantial amount, but look deeper. If you earn 5% on the $1 million, you could generate $50,000 in income each year. As you can see, $1 million in insurance doesn't allow for a great life and it doesn't help you achieve any additional goals. That's why it is critical to identify and assess your *specific* needs.

There are other factors, beyond current income, that play into a partner's needs, should they lose a spouse. For instance, the spouse who is primarily responsible for the kids and the house may not go back to work for an extended period of time, or maybe not at all. Conversely, the primary wage earner may have to hire extra help to care for the house and kids. These are all things that need to be built into the protection program.

When you're ready to purchase a life-insurance policy, consider the source. A lot of people simply buy into the policy offered at their workplace. The problem with this decision is that work policies are only in place for as long as you work there. We recommend buying term insurance to cover this need. A combination of work and private policies can give you the coverage you need for the best price.

Disability of a Wage Earner

You or your spouse sustained an injury that will prevent you from working—and thus, earning a paycheck—for an unknown period of time. For most couples, this is the ultimate nightmare, but with disability insurance, you can ensure your survival and your sanity. However, if you didn't take the time to carefully select the disability policy required by your needs, you may still feel an incredible strain on your finances.

Disability insurance is similar to life insurance, except that the benefits are temporary and the need for it is far more likely. Unlike life insurance, disability benefits are paid on a monthly basis for as long as you are disabled. They are also typically not subject to tax, so the goal is to replace at least 60% of your income. This means that if you earn a salary of $200,000 per year, you would need at least $10,000 per month in disability.

There are many things to consider when selecting a policy. In order to narrow down the type of coverage you need, ask yourself the following questions:

1. What is the definition of disability?
2. How much disability income will you receive?
3. Do you have the maximum amount of disability coverage and can you purchase more in the future as your income increases?
4. Does the policy clearly spell out the definition of disability? Certain policies allow disability coverage if you can't work in your occupation, and others do not pay if you still have the ability to work at *any* job, so be sure to check and see which kind you have.

Personal Liability Lawsuit and Property Damage or Loss

These two risks go hand-in-hand. Why? Because the protection you have against damage or loss can extend to protect you against liability in the event of a true disaster.

It's easy to understand why you would need protection for your home from catastrophic loss, but few realize how vulnerable they are to excess liability.

Umbrella insurance, or excess liability of catastrophe coverage, will protect you in the case of a lawsuit above your homeowners or auto insurance limits. It also protects you if someone is injured on your property. And the best part is that umbrella coverage can easily be added to your existing homeowners policy. Most people never need extended coverage, but when they do, they sure are glad they have it.

Again, how do you choose the best policy? Consider the following questions before deciding which is right for you:

1. Do you have the proper coverage?
2. Have you renewed the coverage to take into account appreciation on your house?
3. Does your homeowners policy include valuable items such as diamonds, artwork, or collectibles?
4. Have you added an umbrella policy to your existing homeowners policy to cover catastrophic losses?

5. Is your umbrella policy coordinated with your auto policy?

Long-Term Sickness of a Family Member

It's unpleasant to think about a loved one falling ill and requiring care, but avoiding the topic will only subject you to greater hardship. In order to avoid exorbitant expenses, and have more power in choosing what happens to your family member, long-term–care insurance will protect you and your loved one.

We often encounter couples with a parent who has been diagnosed with a debilitating illness. The spouse of that parent is unable to care for his or her increasing needs, but neither wants the ill partner to be relocated to a care facility. Long-term–care insurance means that you can afford to provide a caretaker so your parents can live comfortably with the medical assistance they need. It's a blessing, not just for your parents, but for the whole family as well, depending on your assets.

Death Taxes

"Death taxes" is simply a more morbid term for "estate taxes," which basically means that when you pass on, Uncle Sam—and your state—collect a portion of your estate. Planning means that you can ensure your legacy is passed on to those who you elect to receive it. This is a particularly important topic for those who are nearing retirement. We'll go over this subject in depth in the next chapter, but for now know that there are methods to mitigate this financial threat.

Insuring Your Financial Health and Happiness

Insurance is a complex beast with many moving parts. The type of insurance you need may vary, but the amount of insurance you require is non-negotiable. You have vulnerabilities, and those vulnerabilities must be met, plain and simple.

Because of the complexity of insurance policies, we advise you seek out help from an expert who specializes in insurance.

We personally work with highly rated insurance specialists who compare all policies available and select the best one for each of our clients. This specialist lives, breathes, and sleeps insurance policies; he or she understands the intrinsic properties and can help you rest assured that you have the best protection. But remember, most insurance agents earn commission, so ideally, you want an independent and objective analysis of the type and kind of insurance you need before talking to an insurance agent.

And that's the point of all this planning, after all: for you to sleep easy knowing that you're covered.

Once these strategies have been agreed upon, it's time to implement them and return to the things you enjoy in life. But the work is never truly over; if your situation in life changes, so will your needs, which is why it's important to reevaluate your policies after they're in place. This will protect your assets so they are there in the future when you need them most. Safeguarding your assets also means that your retirement is on the right track, all the way to the Legacy™ stage, which is what we'll discuss in the following pages.

CHAPTER 9

Legacy

Estate planning has a bad rap. Mention anything along the lines of "will" or "last wishes" and the party is officially over.

Estate planning is a means to protect and pass on your Legacy, but for many, it's a panic-inducing, taboo subject that must be avoided at all costs—until it's too late.

Let's face it: Few people want to discuss estate planning because it's not fun. Usually, planning means determining how you will achieve your dreams. Estate planning, on the other hand, means you're not going to live forever.

It's time to end the stigma. Because when it comes down to it, estate planning is not about death or mortality; it's about taking care of the people you love.

The primary purpose of estate planning is to be sure that you—and not the state—direct how your assets are to be distributed. By overcoming the anxiety and addressing these sometimes-uncomfortable topics, you can ensure family security, business succession, management of your assets, and the nomination of a guardian for your minor children. You can also ensure that those who inherit your estate won't be burdened with the added costs of fees and taxes later on. It's an important step for your comprehensive financial future. And, if done the right way, it provides wonderful peace of mind.

On the other hand, if estate planning is put off for too long, or if it fails to address commonly overlooked factors, then stress is just the beginning of your problems.

So what's holding you back from ensuring your future?

In part, the culprit is the very world in which we live. Ours is a culture of fear when it comes to anything even hinting at mortality. But that's not the only thing to blame. In fact, many people are unaware of the various ways in which they are affecting the outcome of their legacy.

"I already took care of it."

Perhaps you think you've already got estate planning covered. You wouldn't be alone; most people do. In fact, a majority of people who have drafted a will believe their estate planning is taken care of; everything is coordinated and their objectives will be achieved.

The trouble is, unless you've had the benefit of careful guidance from a financial planner and estate attorney, your wishes may not be carried out in the way you believe your will dictates. Don't get us wrong; it is absolutely wonderful to have a will in place, but it is not the be-all and end-all of estate planning.

If you were tempted to skip over this subject because you believe you already have a plan in place, we encourage you to take another look, with the help of an expert.

"I don't have enough for it to matter."

Another misconception is the belief that you don't have a lot of money, so estate planning is not something you need to worry about. The truth is, even if you don't expect to leave behind an inheritance, there are other things, such as liabilities and final wishes, that must be accounted for.

Chances are, even if you don't leave behind a financial legacy, you will have loved ones who want to honor you in the way you deserve. Creating a plan means that your loved ones will have the gift of guidance in your absence.

"I'm too young."

If you've learned anything in this book, we hope it's that it is never too early to plan for your future. Age is no excuse! For parents and spouses, it is especially important to be proactive about making a plan for your family. The most obvious element of that plan is ensuring your children have a guardian. It can be difficult to decide who will raise and care for them in your absence. A lot of people want to name their parents, but if they are older, it may not be the best choice.

A common mistake when naming guardians is to also name them as the beneficiary of the estate. This is done with the mindset that the guardian will use the money to raise the children. In a perfect world, it would work out this way, but remember, whoever is named as the beneficiary is legally entitled to those funds, and it's ultimately up to him or her to decide what he or she will do with them.

The greatest risk of not having a plan at a young age—or worse, at retirement age— is that, if you don't have a will, the state dictates how your estate is distributed. And often, it's not where you would choose. For instance, in some states, the estate may go to the living parents. This means that even if you're married, if your spouse isn't named in a will, they won't necessarily be cared for in the event of your absence.

You can always change the plan, but by at least having something in writing, you will ensure your loved ones are cared for, no matter what.

"My finances are a mess."

Nobody wants to have company when their house is a mess. When it's your financial house? Even worse. Stress or embarrassment can sometimes be the defining factor that prevents people from securing help to plan their estate. Either their finances are so fragmented that the idea of combing through it all is overwhelming, or they find their lack of organization downright embarrassing.

To all those who might relate: Take a deep breath and relax. Finances are a difficult matter. Even when you're doing your best, if you don't have the extensive knowledge of a professional planner, managing your estate can be a real uphill battle. So go easy on yourself. The only thing you have to fear is missing the opportunity to ensure your wishes are carried out. Don't be embarrassed or intimidated if you don't have your house in order. In fact, many of us find ourselves in that position at some point in our life. The important thing to remember is that the longer you put it off, the further your future is away from you. Any CPA, CFP, or attorney will be happy to provide some advice and the answers you need.

If You're Still Not Convinced

Now that you understand the importance of having a plan in place, it's time to look at key factors that every plan should address. Every person is unique; so, too, are the terms of his or her estate plan. Use the following guidelines as jumping-off points to help you discover your specific needs.

Estate Tax

The estate includes all assets, minus liabilities. People think that liabilities go away after the person is gone, but that's not the case. Instead, they become liabilities of the estate.

The estate tax is a good reason why you should consider gifting to your loved ones while you're still here, plus you have the added bonus of being able to see them enjoy it. When people think of "legacy," they think of monuments and wills. We believe a living legacy is even more rewarding, both for you and for those whom you love.

Big Life Changes

Significant changes in life affect how you'd like your estate to be passed on. A will is not to be kept in a safety-deposit box and never looked at again. Be sure to keep your will current by returning to it every few years and making any necessary updates. Here is a list to help you recognize when it might be time to revise:

- Marriage
- Divorce
- Death of a spouse
- Substantial change in estate size

- Moving to another state or country
- Death of an executor, trustee, or guardian if appointed in the original will
- Birth or adoption
- Serious illness of a family member
- New business or change of business interest
- Retirement
- Change of health
- Purchase of property in another state or country
- Changes in income-tax and estate-tax laws
- Children's marriage
- Children's divorce
- Problem child
- Aging parents
- Special-needs child

Family Feuds

For those who have multiple children, one of the most difficult decisions is deciding how to divide assets. And so to keep things fair, most people divide everything equally. That means something like a vacation house could be split five ways among five siblings.

Although it seems fair, in reality, dividing assets often only leads to family rifts. *Who gets to use the house? Who pays expenses? Who decides when to sell it?* These assets ultimately become problems because they were not discussed beforehand.

A family business is another potential source of turmoil. Some kids are a part of the business; some are not. Those who are not in the business want their fair share, while those running it think the others don't deserve it—even though the will dictates it's divided evenly. Unfortunately, this causes more feuds than achieving the original intention of bringing the family closer together.

Instead of leaving it up to fate, speak with your family. Ask them what they'd like to do with certain things you plan to hand down. Have the conversation while you're here so everyone can voice his or her opinion.

The Loved Ones' Letter

Have you ever been responsible for the estate of a loved one who passed away? If so, you know how challenging it is to juggle such a responsibility during an emotional time.

In most families, one spouse usually handles all of the finances. While this arrangement may have worked swimmingly when both partners were around, it can add up to confusion and anguish in the event of losing that partner. All of a sudden, someone has to track down documents and sort through accounts no one even knew existed.

Unfortunately, people who miss out on the opportunity to plan for this stage also tend to live in the fragmented-finances trap. It all amounts to a paper jungle upon their death, with little way to know if every account and insurance policy will be identified.

The Progression of Wealth stops this fear in its tracks. We've developed a process to take away that stress, and we call it the Loved Ones' Letter.

The Loved Ones' Letter is a tool that you put together, and then put away with the wills. This is a letter to your loved ones that will guide them through your wishes in the event of your death. In it, you include information such as accounts in your name, insurance policies, and more:

Loved Ones' Letter Checklist

- General Information
- Contact Information
- Detailed Banking and Investment Account Information
- Personal Property Listing
- Debts and Obligations
- Insurance Policies
- Employment History
- Summary of Employee Benefits
- Estate-Planning Documents
- Other Pertinent Information
- Burial Wishes and Arrangements

Loved Ones' Letter Template

Dear loved ones,

This letter is a reminder of all of the matters that we have talked about over the years. It should not be construed as my will. A copy of my will is in our safety-deposit box at the bank on the corner of Main Street and 6th Street, and a copy has also been furnished to our financial advisors, Jay Heller and Brian Kohute of Meridian Wealth Partners. They will help advise you and select an attorney for the issues you will be facing during the next year. There is a file in our computer system that lists all of our investments, which is called "Legacy." A more accurate count is directly available from Jay Heller and Brian Kohute.

I have attached to the Loved Ones' Letter a checklist that gives a full description of all the advisors we currently use. However, once again, through The Progression of Wealth Process, Meridian Wealth Partners handles all of this and has been furnished with a copy of this checklist. They are also helping me to prepare the checklist and letter, a process in which you are involved.

The checklist includes a complete listing of all of our assets. I have included here only assets that are not supervised by Meridian Wealth Partners, including our homes. However, they are fully aware of all of our assets except for a few stock certificates that I keep in our safety-deposit box and some savings bonds that are attached to this list. In addition, we have no outstanding liabilities at this time except for some credit cards.

On the insurance-coverage part of the list, I have listed all of the insurance we have, but once again, Meridian Wealth Partners has supervised the insurance policies and has complete information on this. As you know, when we reach 65, we will discontinue our disability policies, so that will not be on the list; however, our long-term–care insurance *will* be listed. Once again, Meridian Wealth Partners will have this information. You will have to make arrangements with our health-insurance company to cancel my benefits. Remember to submit to my employer the Certificate of Death. I have also included a detail of all of the documents that were signed and are all located in our safety-deposit box. Meridian Wealth Partners and our attorney, John Smith, also hold copies.

For general information, I have included—just to make it easier for you—my social security, driver's license, and passport numbers. I have named you and our children, Jack and Morgan, as co-executors of my estate, and as such, you will be responsible for various duties, which John Smith will explain to you. Arrange to see John and Jay after the funeral so that you can start the probate of the will without delay. Your income should be more than accurate based on The Progression of Wealth planning; however, once again, these are events where you need to redo The Progression of Wealth Blueprint and The Progression of Wealth Process. You do not need to rush into this; however, you should begin this process within two months and I'm sure Jay or Brian will contact you to do this. I do believe that you and the children are adequately provided for and will be well taken care of. The title to our homes is in both of our names and will pass to you outside the probate court. The deed is in our safety-deposit box.

I have enclosed a checklist of my final wishes. I love you and the children, and hope that during this trying time, this letter makes it a little easier for you.

Love,

****

The Greatest Gift

The Loved Ones' Letter is one of the easiest tools in The Progression of Wealth, but often, the hardest to complete because of its emotional subject matter.

We encourage you to think ahead and put into writing your wishes for those you will leave behind. This is never easy, but it will take the burden off those whom you love when they must make tough decisions during their time of grief.

Use our template to help guide you throughout your process. Once you complete the letter, be sure that each family member has a copy that can be easily located. Remember, planning ahead is one of the greatest gifts you could give to your family. This letter is a wonderful document that will allow your loved ones to honor your legacy in the way that you deserve.

CHAPTER 10

Make It Happen Today

We've outlined the journey of planning for your financial future. We've made the case for how and why you can live the retirement of your dreams, and we've gone through The Progression of Wealth process—except for one step: action.

Yes, it's time to take action. Take action to provide for your loved ones. Take action to ensure your retirement is everything you want it to be. Take action to pave the path to your independence, where your finances work for you.

You know how critical it is to have a plan in order to fulfill your retirement goals, both financial and personal. Without a plan, your dreams of spending summers on the shore, gifting to your favorite charity, or living comfortably in your beautiful home with your partner hang in the balance. Perhaps that's the reason why you picked up this book: You appreciate the value of planning. The process of creating a plan, and then carrying it out, however, that's another story.

But now, after following us through these pages, you have the plan that will bridge the gap between dream and reality: You have The Progression of Wealth.

To review all that you've learned, let's take a look at the steps we've outlined along the way:

Having Stability Means Having a Plan

We live in a world of uncertainties. Our world does not reward chance, but rather, strategic planning and action. By acknowledging this essential fact, you have begun your journey through The Progression of Wealth.

Dream About Your Retirement— and Dream Big

Without dreams and desires, there's no need for a plan. Dream big about what you want your retirement to look like. OK, so maybe "flying to the moon" might be a little extravagant, but we find that most goals are achievable with the right amount of planning and dedication. As you move through the process, you'll discover which dreams are important to you, and which don't fit the overall picture.

Get your partner in on the discussion. If you haven't already, this is the time to discuss everything you want to achieve, both separately and as a couple. In this early stage, it is important to write down everything that comes to mind. This helps to prioritize your most important goals and set appropriate timelines.

Fragmented-Finances, Be Gone!

Fragmented finances occur when you have multiple accounts with multiple advisors and no idea how everything is working together (or not). Fragmented finances is the number-one hang-up that prevents people from achieving their financial goals. Even worse, fragmented finances don't end with you; if they're not dealt with, your scattered state of affairs becomes the most stressful gift you could ever pass on your loved ones.

People fall into this trap because they believe that by spreading their finances across institutions and advisors, they are mitigating risk. Really, they are only creating more risk.

The solution? Consolidate your finances. Find one advisor to carry the torch and guide you to success. The following steps show you how to create your plan:

1. Draft the Blueprint

Once you've decided on an advisor and have begun the process of dreaming up your future, it's time to get down to business. Draw up the plan for your very own Progression of Wealth.

As you know, the Blueprint takes into account the following life goals:
1. Helping and protecting your family
2. Enjoying and protecting your lifestyle
3. Planning for the expected and unexpected
4. Building a legacy
5. Creating financial comfort

With the Blueprint in hand, these dreams are no longer fantasies—they are a part of your future.

2. Build the Foundation

Your financial foundation comprises two parts: one, your current financial situation, and, two, your future financial goals.

The Roman philosopher Seneca once wrote, "Luck is what happens when preparation meets opportunity."

Wealth is what happens when the Foundation meets the Blueprint. With this combination of goals and a comprehensive analysis of your current finances, you will be well on your way to the retirement of your dreams.

3. *Declare Your Financial Independence*

This stage provides you with verifiable evidence that the goals and methods you've set forth for achieving them will indeed turn out as planned. If necessary, this is the stage when the plan will be tweaked to account for future factors that may impact your goals.

4. *Choose the Right Investments*

Investments are the best way to beat inflation and ensure your money will work for you at the time when you need it. There are many myths that go along with investing, and perhaps the most common is that investing is too risky. While it's true that there is risk involved, it is within your control to manage your level of risk. And, of course, in the long run, your investments should grow.

5. *Protect Your Assets and Your Family*

Once you have your financial Blueprint in place, and you've used tools to determine the plan will work for you, there are other areas in your life that require your attention. Some of these items might be clear at the onset; others may become apparent later on in life. It's important to be aware of the tools available to you, such as long-term–care insurance, to protect your assets, as well as your loved ones.

6. Leaving a Legacy

You've put a lot of hard work into planning your estate, all with the goal of living the retirement you choose, not the one you are left with, as well as being able to provide for those whom you love. Tools such as the Loved Ones' Letter will guide your loved ones, and provide peace of mind for the family, no matter what happens.

7. Same Time, Next Year

While The Progression of Wealth was designed to take the guesswork and worry out of your future, it does not remove the unpredictable factors of life. After you put the plan in motion, check back in to see your progress. Not only will it be a proud moment for you to see how far you've come, but you will also have the power to adjust your plan if anything has changed.

To Win the Race, You Need the Right Coach

We've provided the tools that will guide you in forming your plan; it is now up to you to make use of them. Don't live another minute in the fragmented-finances trap. Don't waste another second leaving your legacy at risk of becoming the government's legacy.

Use The Progression of Wealth process.

Think of yourself as a track runner. You are the one who will train countless hours to build up your strength and endurance. When it comes time for the big race, you are the one who will dig your spikes into the ground and make it past the finish line. But without your coach to guide you through workouts, teach you technique, and keep you motivated through injury, where would you be?

The Progression of Wealth is your own race; an advisor will coach you across the finish line. An advisor will utilize your unique talents and skills, and combine them with his or her wisdom to do what it takes to win the retirement of your dreams.

So who can you call to guide you through this process?

We've touched on how to find an advisor who is right for you earlier in the book. Now, let's take a look at what an advisor should provide for you, now that you have a better understanding of the plan you need.

Whether you're an individual, a couple, or a participant in an employee retirement plan, your advisor should strive to make sure you are financially prepared to live the retirement you envisioned.

When we talk about how to find the right advisor for you, we inevitably look at how he or she might measure up to our own firm. Some may consider it boastful; we simply consider it sound reason. We can say this with confidence because we have a very high client-satisfaction and retention rate.

Our firm exists solely because we saw what other so-called advisors were doing, and we didn't like it. We knew we could do better by offering truly comprehensive planning to our clients to help them meet their goals. Unlike many other firms that make their living by selling products, we avoid conflicts of interest when we recommend this or that product. This independence allows us to act in our clients' best interests when we make recommendations.

We are 100% conflict-free to help *you* design the plan that's best for *you*, which is why our clients stick with us. They get acclimated to an entirely different level of experience than they have had with previous financial advisors—and they never want to go back!

We are committed to serving clients with diligence and integrity by applying our proprietary process for comprehensive wealth management. Yes, it is more labor intensive, but we feel it serves our clients' full needs for effective retirement planning. We're not interested in doing anything less, and you should expect the same from your advisor.

If you are interested in seeking guidance for the next steps, we are happy to help. Let us show you how to solve the dilemma of fragmented finances and offer clarity, insight, and partnership in order to ensure that you will reach your financial and retirement goals. Let us take away the stress and worry of worrying whether or not you will have enough to maintain your lifestyle through retirement.

Our goal is to make your life better with our proven strategy of wealth management, and to create a partnership in which, together, we will walk through the progress of building your wealth.

Using our Progression of Wealth process, we will help you plan and invest so you are prepared for the expected *and* unexpected in retirement.

Whether it is with our firm, or with another trusted advisor, create a plan to walk through your Progression of Wealth with someone you can trust to help you now, along your path, and into retirement. Build a partnership with someone who understands you and your goals, and who is committed to assisting you in maintaining your desired lifestyle, or who will help you map out a strategy for a whole new future.

About the Authors

Jay Heller

Jay Heller, a Managing Director of Meridian Wealth Partners, LLC, is co-author of **The Progression of Wealth**®, a book he wrote with partner Brian Kohute to explain their trademarked methodology of wealth management for high-net-worth families.

Jay began his career as a CPA advising business owners. He is a Personal Financial Specialist (PFS), a designation available only to CPAs meeting specific requirements and passing exams authorized by the American Institute of Certified Public Accountants. Only about 7,000 of the nation's 400,000 CPAs have met the requirements.

Jay, who has more than 35 years of experience as a financial advisor, is a sought-after speaker at seminars for financial professionals and is annually named on Philadelphia's Five Star Wealth Manager List. Jay is often quoted in consumer media outlets including Kiplinger's Personal Finance, MarketWatch. com, and CNN, as well as in industry publications such as Accounting Today, CPA Wealth Provider, and Investment News. Outside of helping clients achieve their financial goals, Jay enjoys his time with his wife, Randi, and their kids and grandchildren.

Brian Kohute

Brian Kohute is a Managing Director of Meridian Wealth Partners, LLC. He oversees all portfolio management and investment research activities. With more than 25 years of experience in working with business owners, high-net-worth families, and corporate executives, Brian develops, implements, and monitors the firm's Progression of Wealth solutions.

In addition to being a CPA and PFS, Brian is also a Chartered Financial Analyst (CFA). The CFA designation is a globally recognized standard for measuring the competence and integrity of investment professionals. To obtain the CFA charter, candidates must successfully complete three difficult exams and gain at least three years of qualifying work experience, among other requirements. In passing these exams, candidates demonstrate their competence, integrity, and extensive knowledge in accounting, ethical and professional standards, economics, portfolio management and security analysis. While the vast majority of CFA professionals work as research analysts for Wall Street firms, Brian is one of a growing cadre of CFAs who took the three-year education program and passed the three-part exam to apply his investment knowledge to serving high-net-worth families.

Brian is consistently named a Philadelphia Five Star Wealth Manager, and is also a host of a local cable TV show, Money Matters, which has aired on the Comcast Cable System for the past ten years. He has been happily married for fifteen years to his wife, Michelle, and they are enjoying raising their two boys, Gavin and Liam.

CPSIA information can be obtained
at www.ICGtesting.com
Printed in the USA
BVOW10*1403240817
492534BV00003B/3/P